United States Government Accountability Office

Report to Congressional Committees

January 2012

DEFENSE CONTRACTING

Improved Policies and Tools Could Help Increase Competition on DOD's National Security Exception Procurements

GAO
Accountability ★ Integrity ★ Reliability

GAO-12-263

G A O
Accountability * Integrity * Reliability

Highlights

Highlights of GAO-12-263, a report to congressional committees

DEFENSE CONTRACTING

Improved Policies and Tools Could Help Increase Competition on DOD's National Security Exception Procurements

Why GAO Did This Study

Competition is a critical tool for achieving the best return on the government's investment. Federal agencies are generally required to award contracts competitively, but they are permitted to use other than full and open competition in certain situations, such as when open competition would reveal information that would harm national security. GAO examined DOD's use of this provision, known as the national security exception. It requires the use of competition to the greatest extent practicable. GAO assessed (1) the pattern of DOD's use of the national security exception; (2) DOD's processes for using the exception; and (3) the extent to which DOD achieved competition under the exception. GAO analyzed federal procurement data; reviewed a selection of 27 contract files and justifications citing the exception from the Army, Navy, and Air Force, based on largest obligations, frequent users, and a range of procurement types, as well as five contracts from DOD intelligence agencies; and interviewed DOD contracting and program officials.

What GAO Recommends

GAO recommends that DOD issue guidance clarifying when security sensitive contracting data must be reported, monitor the impact of new Air Force class justification processes, and consider using tools that facilitate market research in a secure environment. DOD concurred with two recommendations and partially concurred with the recommendation on clarifying guidance, citing pending revisions to regulations. GAO continues to believe that clarifying guidance is needed.

View GAO-12-263. For more information, contact Belva Martin at (202) 512-4841 or martinb@gao.gov.

What GAO Found

DOD's use of the national security exception is small—about 2 percent of the dollar value of its total use of exceptions to full and open competition, but gaps in federal procurement data limit GAO's ability to determine the full extent of DOD's use. DOD procures a range of goods and services under this exception, and according to federal procurement data, the Air Force accounted for about 74 percent of DOD's use during fiscal years 2007 through 2010. However, DOD intelligence agencies and special access programs frequently use the exception, but are generally excluded from reporting procurement data. While an Office of the Secretary of Defense memorandum exempts three of the intelligence agencies from reporting such data, DOD policy on reporting sensitive procurements for other military department programs is not clear.

For most national security exception contract actions GAO reviewed, DOD used a single justification and approval document that applies to multiple contracts— known as a class justification. Among those reviewed, $3.3 billion of $3.4 billion was obligated under contracts that used class justifications, which reduce the steps required to proceed with individual contract actions that do not use full and open competition. According to contracting officials, the increased flexibility of national security exception class justifications helps meet mission needs. However, in the Air Force, concerns about the reduced management review of these contracts have led to changes in the process for approving individual contract actions using class justifications. Nevertheless, all of the justifications GAO reviewed met Federal Acquisition Regulation requirements.

GAO's analysis of federal procurement data on about 11,300 contract actions found that, from fiscal years 2007 through 2010, only 16 percent of all obligations under those actions by the military departments under the national security exception received more than one proposal, as shown in the figure below. Contract files and contracting officials cited a limited pool of companies with the right capabilities, the difficulty of changing from an established vendor, and limited tools for soliciting competitive bids as reasons for their inability to obtain more competition. Twelve of the 27 military department contract files GAO reviewed did not include a record of market research, and others included few details on the results. Two intelligence agencies that reported using the national security exception for all contracting reported achieving comparatively high levels of competition. Both have systems that catalogue firms, capabilities, and solicitations that are used to facilitate security sensitive market research.

Number of Offers Received on Armed Service National Security Exception Contracts by Percentage of Dollars Obligated, Fiscal Years 2007 through 2010

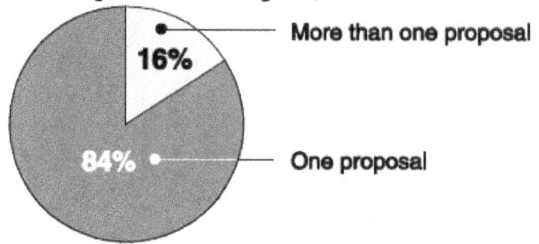

Source: GAO analysis of FPDS-NG data.

_____ United States Government Accountability Office

Contents

Abbreviations

ACC	Army Contracting Command
AFMC	Air Force Materiel Command
AMC	Army Materiel Command
ARC	Acquisition Research Center or Acquisition Resource Center
CICA	Competition in Contracting Act
DIA	Defense Intelligence Agency
DOD	Department of Defense
DPAP	Defense Procurement and Acquisition Policy
FAR	Federal Acquisition Regulation
FPDS-NG	Federal Procurement Data System-Next Generation
IG	Inspector General
NGA	National Geospatial-Intelligence Agency
NRO	National Reconnaissance Office
NSA	National Security Agency
NSE	National Security Exception
OSD	Office of the Secretary of Defense
SAP	Special Access Programs
SMDC	Space and Missile Defense Command
SPAWAR	Space and Naval Warfare Systems Command

United States Government Accountability Office
Washington, DC 20548

January 13, 2012

Congressional Committees

The Department of Defense (DOD) spent an average of $370 billion per year buying goods and services during fiscal years 2007 through 2010. The Federal Acquisition Regulation (FAR) requires, with limited exceptions, that contracting officers promote and provide for full and open competition in soliciting offers and awarding contracts. One exception—the national security exception—allows agencies to limit potential offerors on a contract solicitation in instances when disclosure of the agency's needs would compromise national security, but still requires agencies to request offers from as many potential sources as practicable. DOD's Better Buying Power initiative, launched in September 2010, recognized that DOD has not taken full advantage of opportunities for competition to achieve the best possible return on its investments.

The National Defense Authorization Act for Fiscal Year 2011 mandated that we review DOD's use of the national security exception. The mandate required us to review (1) the pattern of usage of such exception by acquisition organizations within the department to determine which organizations are commonly using the exception and the frequency of such usage; (2) the range of items or services being acquired through the use of such exception; (3) the process for reviewing and approving justifications involving such exception; (4) whether the justifications for use of such exception typically meet the requirements of the FAR applicable to the use of such exception; (5) issues associated with follow-on procurements for items or services acquired using such exception; and (6) potential additional instances where such exception could be applied and any authorities available to the department other than such exception that could be applied in such instances.[1] To answer the mandate, we (1) identified the pattern of DOD's use of the national security exception to full and open competition, including the range of goods and services acquired; (2) assessed DOD's process for using this exception; and (3) determined the extent to which DOD obtained competition on selected contracts when using the national security exception. To determine

---

[1] Ike Skelton National Defense Authorization Act for Fiscal Year 2011, Pub. L. No. 111-383, § 844 (b).

GAO-12-263 Defense Contracting

DOD's pattern of use of the national security exception, we analyzed data from the Federal Procurement Data System – Next Generation (FPDS-NG) for fiscal years 2007 through 2010, and obtained data on competition and use of this exception from the DOD intelligence agencies. We determined that the federal procurement data for these fiscal years were sufficiently reliable to identify DOD's use of the national security exception, in part by verifying a non-generalizable random sample of the data from the Army, Navy, and Air Force (referred to throughout this report as the military departments). To determine DOD's processes for using this exception, we used federal procurement data to select a non-generalizable sample of 27 contract files at the military departments based on largest obligations, frequent users, and a range of procurement types. In addition, we reviewed five contracts provided by DOD intelligence agencies, for a total of 32 contracts across DOD as a whole.[2] We did not include other DOD entities in our sample that reported little or no use of the exception in federal procurement data. We analyzed the documents the military departments and intelligence agencies used to seek approval to limit competition on the selected contracts and determined whether they met the requirements of the FAR. We conducted legal research and interviewed DOD officials on other uses of the exception and alternative authorities. Furthermore, we analyzed policies and guidance, federal procurement data, and met with DOD officials at the Office of the Secretary of Defense (OSD), the three military departments, and four DOD intelligence agencies. To determine the extent to which DOD obtained competition under the national security exception, we reviewed the 32 selected military department and intelligence agency contract files, and analyzed FPDS-NG data on the number of proposals received for contracts awarded using this exception. With military department and intelligence agency officials, we also discussed efforts DOD makes to obtain competition when using the national security exception as its authority to limit competition.

A more detailed description of our scope and methodology is presented in appendix I. We conducted this performance audit from March 2011 to January 2012 in accordance with generally accepted government auditing standards. Those standards require that we plan and perform the audit to obtain sufficient, appropriate evidence to provide a reasonable basis for

---

[2] Because we did not have a list of intelligence agency contract numbers from which to choose, we relied on the agencies to select the contracts for review.

our findings and conclusions based on our audit objectives. We believe that the evidence obtained provides a reasonable basis for our findings and conclusions based on our audit objectives.

Background

The FAR requires that contracting officers provide for full and open competition in soliciting proposals and awarding government contracts. However, the FAR also recognizes that full and open competition is not always feasible, and authorizes contracting without full and open competition under certain conditions. Situations for which the FAR provides exceptions include[3]

- only one responsible source and no other supplies or services will satisfy agency requirements;
- unusual and compelling urgency;
- industrial mobilization; engineering, developmental, or research capability; or expert services;
- international agreement;
- authorized or required by statute;
- national security; and
- public interest.

The national security exception allows agencies to limit competition for a contract when the disclosure of the agency's needs would compromise national security—not merely because the acquisition is classified or because access to classified materials is necessary. Further, the national security exception requires that agencies request offers from as many potential sources as practicable, although sole-source awards are permitted. DOD is the largest user of the national security exception, and a variety of entities within the department use the exception.

In September 2010, DOD launched its Better Buying Power initiative, which among other goals, aims to promote effective competition in government contracting. As a result, promoting competition is a focus at DOD, according to a Defense Procurement and Acquisition Policy (DPAP) official, the office within OSD responsible for tracking DOD-wide procurement and competition metrics. As part of these efforts, DPAP

---

[3] The Competition in Contracting Act of 1984 (CICA), Pub. L. 98-369, established these seven exceptions to competition, which are often referred to as CICA exceptions. Subpart 6.3 of the FAR implements the CICA exceptions.

holds quarterly meetings with competition advocates, who are officials designated to promote competition within DOD components.

Generally, noncompetitive contracts must be supported by written justification and approval documents that contain sufficient facts and rationale to justify the use of the specific exception to full and open competition that is being applied to the procurement. These justifications must include, at a minimum, 12 elements specified by the FAR, as shown in table 1.[4]

Table 1: Elements of a Justification for Other Than Full and Open Competition Required by the FAR

Required justification elements
Identification of the agency and the contracting activity, and specific identification of the document as a "justification for other than full and open competition"
Nature and/or description of the action being approved
Description of the supplies or services required to meet the agency's needs, including the estimated value
Identification of the statutory authority permitting other than full and open competition
Demonstration that the proposed contractor's unique qualifications or the nature of the acquisition requires use of the authority cited
Description of efforts made to ensure that offers are solicited from as many potential sources as is practicable, including whether a synopsis of the contract was or will be publicized and, if not, which exception under 5.202 applies
Determination by the contracting officer that the anticipated cost to the government will be fair and reasonable
Description of the market research conducted and the results of the research or a statement as to why market research was not conducted
Any other facts supporting the use of other than full and open competition, such as an explanation why technical data packages, engineering descriptions, statements of work suitable for full and open competition have not been developed or are not available
A listing of the sources, if any, that expressed, in writing, an interest in the acquisition
Statement of the actions, if any, the agency may take to remove or overcome any barriers to competition before subsequent acquisitions for the supplies or services are required
Contracting officer certification that the justification is accurate and complete to the best of the officer's knowledge and belief

Source: FAR § 6.303-2(b).

---

[4] See FAR § 6.303-2 (b) and FAR Subpart 6.304 for approval levels.

The level of the official who must approve a justification is determined by the estimated total dollar value of the contract or contracts to which it will apply, as outlined in the FAR. The approval levels range from the local contracting officer for relatively small contract actions up to the agencywide senior procurement executive for contracts worth more than $85.5 million. The justifications can be made on an individual or class basis; a class justification generally covers programs or sets of programs and has a dollar limit and time period for all actions taken under the authority. The approval levels for the class justification are the same as those for an individual justification and are determined by the total estimated value of the class. Approval of individual contract actions under a class justification requires the contracting officer to ensure that each action taken under it is within the scope of the class justification.

DOD's Use of the National Security Exception Covers a Range of Goods and Services, but Gaps in Data Limit Ability to Determine Full Extent of Use

DOD Military Departments' Use of the National Security Exception Is Small Relative to Other Competition Exceptions and Covers a Range of Goods and Services

Based on data from FPDS-NG, DOD dollar obligations under the national security exception during fiscal years 2007 through 2010 were small relative to other exceptions to full and open competition. Out of the nearly $1.5 trillion that DOD obligated for all contracts during this period, 41 percent ($606.3 billion), were based on other than full and open competition, primarily through the seven FAR exceptions.[5] However, only about $13 billion—or about 2 percent of DOD's other than full and open competition obligations—were obligated under the national security exception. As figure 1 shows, the most common FAR exception used by DOD is "only one responsible source," while other exceptions are used much less frequently.

---

[5] The FAR allows for limited competition in some other instances beyond the seven CICA exceptions, such as actions at or below the Micro-Purchase threshold (FAR Subpart 13.2) or when simplified acquisition procedures are used (FAR Subpart 13.3). These make up less than half a percent of all obligations based on other than full and open competition.

Figure 1: Percentage of Total DOD Obligations Based on Other Than Full and Open Competition, by FAR Exceptions to Competition, Fiscal Years 2007 through 2010

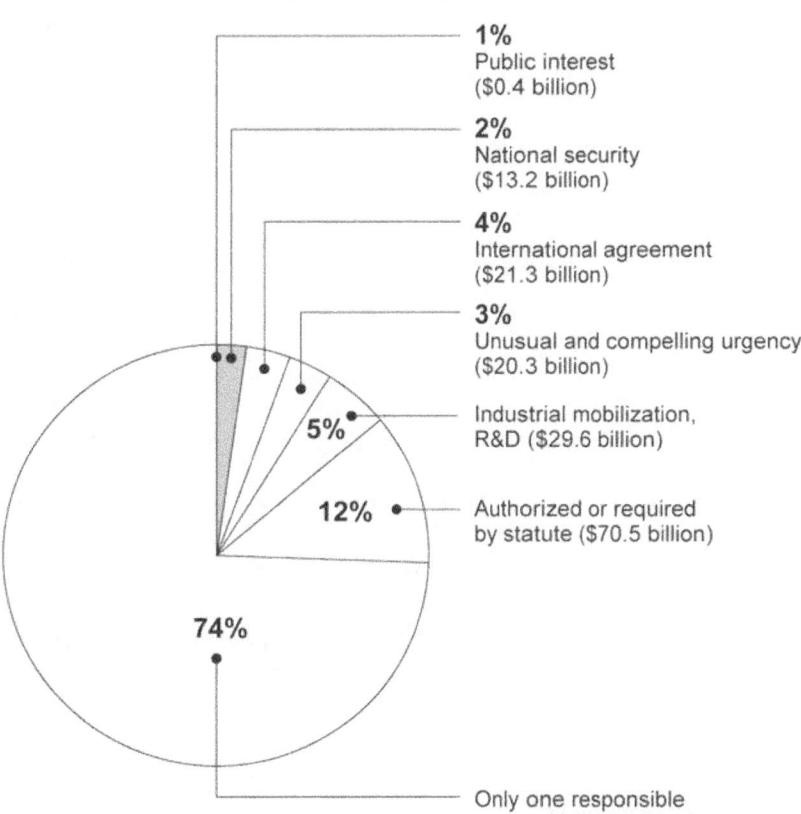

1%
Public interest
($0.4 billion)

2%
National security
($13.2 billion)

4%
International agreement
($21.3 billion)

3%
Unusual and compelling urgency
($20.3 billion)

Industrial mobilization,
R&D ($29.6 billion)

Authorized or required
by statute ($70.5 billion)

Only one responsible
source ($448.6 billion)

5%

12%

74%

Source: GAO analysis of FPDS-NG data.

The three military departments were the largest users of the national security exception during fiscal years 2007 through 2010, according to the data reported in FPDS-NG, obligating about $12.7 billion. The Air Force made up 73.5 percent of all of DOD's obligations under the exception, despite only accounting for about 18 percent of DOD's total contract obligations during the same time period, as figure 2 illustrates. By contrast, non-military-department components accounted for about 4 percent of DOD's use under the exception.

Figure 2: Percentage of National Security Exception Obligations by DOD
Component, Fiscal Years 2007 through 2010

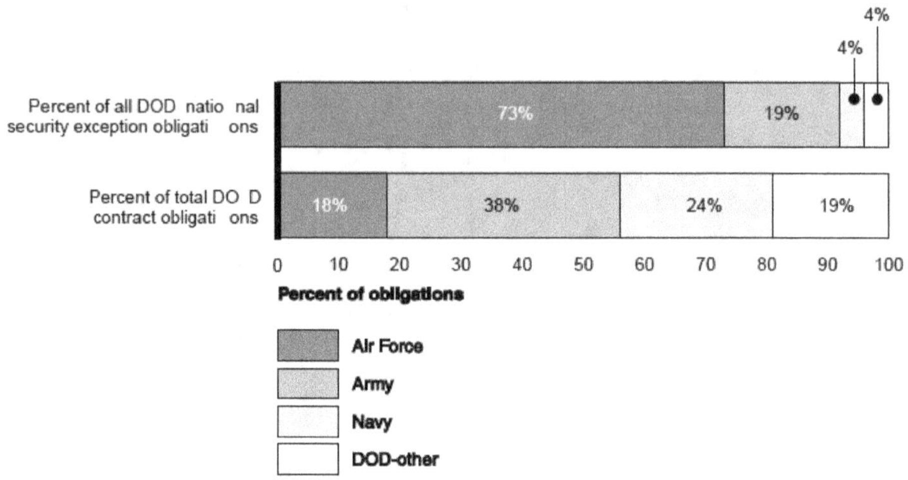

Source: GAO analysis of FPDS-NG data.

During the same 4-year period, over 40 percent of DOD's total obligations
under the national security exception were for services, 37 percent for
supplies and equipment, and about 22 percent for research and
development, as shown in figure 3.

Figure 3: Types of Procurements under the National Security Exception, Fiscal Years 2007 through 2010

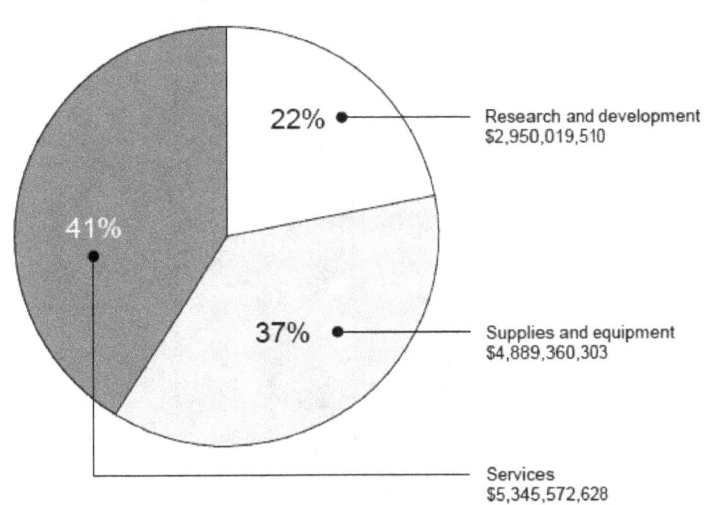

22% ● Research and development
$2,950,019,510

41%

37% ● Supplies and equipment
$4,889,360,303

Services
$5,345,572,628

Source: GAO analysis of FPDS-NG data.

Based on our analysis of FPDS-NG data, the military departments' use of the exception varied both in the extent of use and the types of goods and services acquired. During fiscal years 2007 through 2010, the Air Force obligated $9.7 billion using the national security exception, nearly all by the Air Force Materiel Command. About half of the Air Force's obligations under the national security exception were for services, such as logistical support and professional services, and the other half was primarily for supplies and equipment, such as communication equipment and aircraft components. The second largest user, the Army, obligated $2.5 billion, mostly by the Army Materiel Command and the Space and Missile Defense Command. More than 80 percent of the Army's obligations under the exception were for research and development, mainly in space and missile systems and electronics and communication equipment. Finally, the Navy obligated almost $0.5 billion over the 4 fiscal years under the exception, mostly under Space and Naval Warfare Systems Command contracts. More than half of the Navy's obligations under the exception were to procure services, such as transportation and repair services. Figure 4 shows the percent of obligations represented by each category of procurement within the military departments.

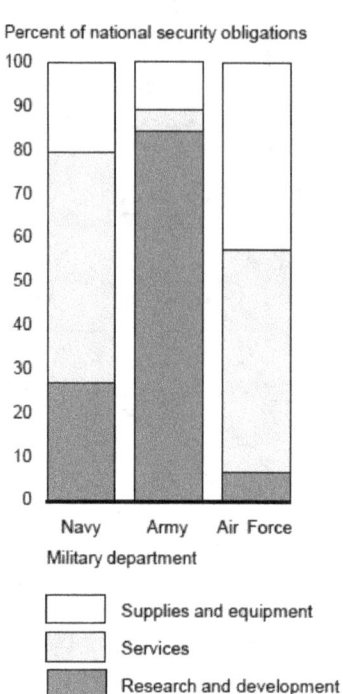

Figure 4: Types of Procurements under the National Security Exception, by Military Department, Fiscal Years 2007 through 2010

Percent of national security obligations

Military department

Supplies and equipment

Services

Research and development

Source: GAO analysis of FPDS-NG data.

DOD Intelligence Agencies and Special Access Programs Use the Exception but Generally Do Not Report Its Use

DOD intelligence agencies often use the national security exception when contracting for supplies and services, but generally do not report contracting data to the OSD or to FPDS-NG. Two of the four DOD intelligence agencies—the National Reconnaissance Office (NRO) and the National Security Agency (NSA)—report using the exception for all their contracting activities. The other two intelligence agencies—the National Geospatial-Intelligence Agency (NGA) and the Defense Intelligence Agency (DIA)—reported using the exception for less than 10 percent of their total contracted obligations.[6] Three of the intelligence

---

[6] DOD intelligence agencies provided the percent of total obligations for their organizations, rather than dollar amounts, as we did not have access to such information. Three of these agencies reported their use for fiscal years 2007 through 2010, but due to database limitations, DIA reported its use only for fiscal year 2010.

agencies, NGA, DIA, and NSA, are exempt from reporting to FPDS-NG based on a memorandum from OSD. NRO is not covered by the memorandum, but also does not appear in FPDS-NG data. However, some of these agencies report overall competition statistics to OSD and participate in DOD-wide competition advocate meetings.[7]

In addition to the intelligence agencies, DOD Special Access Programs (SAP) use the national security exception, but generally do not report data to FPDS-NG.[8] These are specially classified programs within the military departments and other DOD components that limit information to individuals with an explicit need to know. These programs impose safeguarding and access measures beyond those typically taken for information with the same classification level, such as secret and top secret. Most officials told us that, in general, these programs do not report data to FPDS-NG. Therefore, determining the extent to which these entities use the national security exception is not feasible due to the limited access these programs allow. However, like the DOD intelligence agencies, officials at one military department told us that they report overall competition statistics for SAP contracts to DOD. Specifically, Army Contracting Command officials who oversee SAP programs reported that they use the national security exception for nearly all contracting activity and they provide overall obligation totals and competition data to OSD.

DOD Lacks Clear Policy on Reporting Sensitive Contracting Activity

Classified data on contracts, agreements, and orders are excluded from being reported in FPDS-NG. However, DOD does not have a clear policy for excluding sensitive contracting data from being reported in FPDS-NG.[9] While the memorandum from OSD exempts three of DOD's intelligence agencies (NGA, DIA, and NSA) from reporting procurement data to FPDS-NG because of the sensitive nature of their procurement

---

[7] OSD holds quarterly meetings with competition advocates from DOD's 21 different components to discuss ways to increase competition. The intelligence agencies are not required to attend, but OSD officials told us that some participate in the discussions.

[8] DOD distinguishes between two basic types of Special Access Programs—acknowledged and unacknowledged. The unacknowledged programs limit the number of people aware of the program's existence, while acknowledged programs limit the specific details of the programs not the knowledge of the program itself.

[9] For purposes of this report, we define sensitive contract data as data that while not classified, its release could have a negative impact on the agency's ability to perform its mission.

data, OSD and military department officials were not aware of a specific policy basis for excluding sensitive programs outside of the intelligence agencies. In addition to the exclusion of SAP procurement data, some DOD officials told us that contracts outside of SAP do not appear in FPDS-NG due to security concerns. Nevertheless, it appears based on the contracts in our review that the information that is in FPDS-NG on contracting activities using the national security exception is generally from programs that are sensitive but not fully classified programs. Some DOD officials, including at the OSD level, were unaware that some individual contracts could be excluded from FPDS-NG. By contrast, other officials expected all contracts using the national security exception to be excluded from FPDS due to the sensitive nature of the procurements. As a result, it is unclear the extent to which contracting information on SAPs and other highly sensitive contracting activities in DOD are included in FPDS-NG. Based on our review, it appears that most information on such programs is excluded. Further, according to DOD officials, decisions are made on a case-by-case basis to exclude individual contracts from FPDS-NG, but they were unsure of the policy basis for these exclusions.

DOD Often Uses a Single Document to Justify Multiple Actions under the National Security Exception, and All Justifications Met Requirements

DOD Makes Extensive Use of Class Justifications for the National Security Exception

For most contracts we reviewed, DOD entities used a single justification and approval document that applies to multiple contracts—referred to in the FAR as a class justification—for national security exception contract actions. Of the 27 contracts we reviewed at the military departments, all 18 Air Force contracts cited class justifications, as did 4 of the 6 Army contracts. The 2 remaining Army contracts and all 3 Navy contracts we reviewed cited individual justifications. Among the contracts we reviewed, $3.3 billion in obligations during the period of fiscal years 2007 through 2010 used class justifications, while less than $0.1 billion was obligated during that period under individual justifications. Figure 5 shows the relationship between the individual contract files we reviewed and the type of justification used to support the national security exception, as well as the obligation amounts associated with each during this period.[10]

---

[10] One Army contract originally awarded under the national security exception was modified in 2004 to cite the "only one source" exception, and thus had no obligations under the national security exception during the fiscal year 2007 through 2010 period.

Figure 5: Relationship of Contracts Reviewed to Type of Justifications Used by the Military Departments and Associated Obligations for Fiscal Years 2007 - 2010

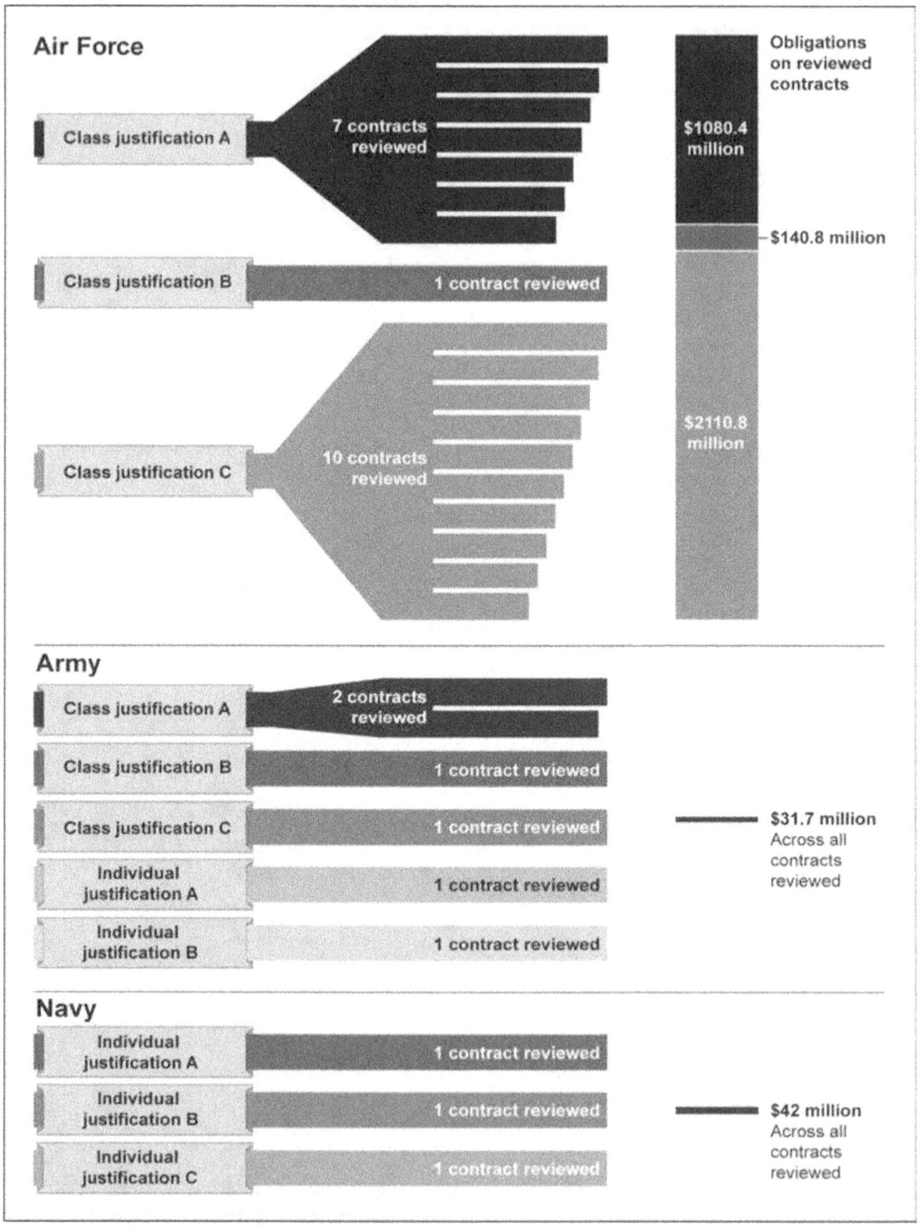

Source: GAO analysis of DOD contract files and FPDS-NG data.
Note: Justifications are noted by generic identifiers, rather than program names.

GAO-12-263 Defense Contracting

The Air Force Materiel Command (AFMC) comprises the majority of the Air Force's use of the national security exception—about 72 percent of DOD's total contract obligations under the exception as reported in FPDS-NG compared to 73.5 percent for the Air Force overall. Officials at the two AFMC centers that make up the majority of the command's contracting under this exception reported that they cite class justifications for the vast majority of their national security exception contracting. The Air Force justifications we reviewed confirmed this, each covering contracts related to multiple systems within a program office. For example, one Air Force class justification had an obligation ceiling of about $8.7 billion for a 7-year period. The Army's class justifications also covered multiple contracts, but were more focused on an individual system within the program office, and two of the three we reviewed had much lower obligation ceilings.

Some of the intelligence agencies also use class justifications for the national security exception. NSA and NRO have class justifications that cover all of their contracting activity. NGA and DIA, by contrast, reported using individual justifications for contracts where they cite the national security exception.

Class justifications reduce the steps required to proceed with individual contract actions that are not fully competitive. Each justification, individual or class, must be approved through the same process, with levels of approval specified by the FAR based on dollar value. However, once a class justification has been approved, the process for individual contract actions changes—an individual contract within the scope of the class justification can generally be approved for limited competition or sole-source award by the local procuring activity, as long as the amount is within the obligation ceiling of the justification. For instance, the Air Force obligated $915 million under an indefinite delivery/indefinite quantity contract for support and modification services on an existing aircraft and its related systems. Because this procurement was within the scope of a national security exception class justification, under the processes established in the FAR, the program office did not have to obtain approval for this noncompetitive acquisition from the Air Force's senior procurement executive.

According to contracting officials at an Air Force program office that has a class justification in place under the national security exception, the increased flexibility of their national security exception class justification helps them meet mission needs. In the absence of a class justification, approval of an individual justification for a noncompetitive contract award takes time; officials with one program office cited an instance of an individual justification under a different FAR exception that was not yet approved 7 months after it was initiated. Figure 6 illustrates the review process for contract awards of $85.5 million or more under class and individual justifications.

Figure 6: Review Process Required by FAR for Approval of Other-Than-Full-and-Open Competition Contract Award over $85.5 Million under a Class or Individual Justification

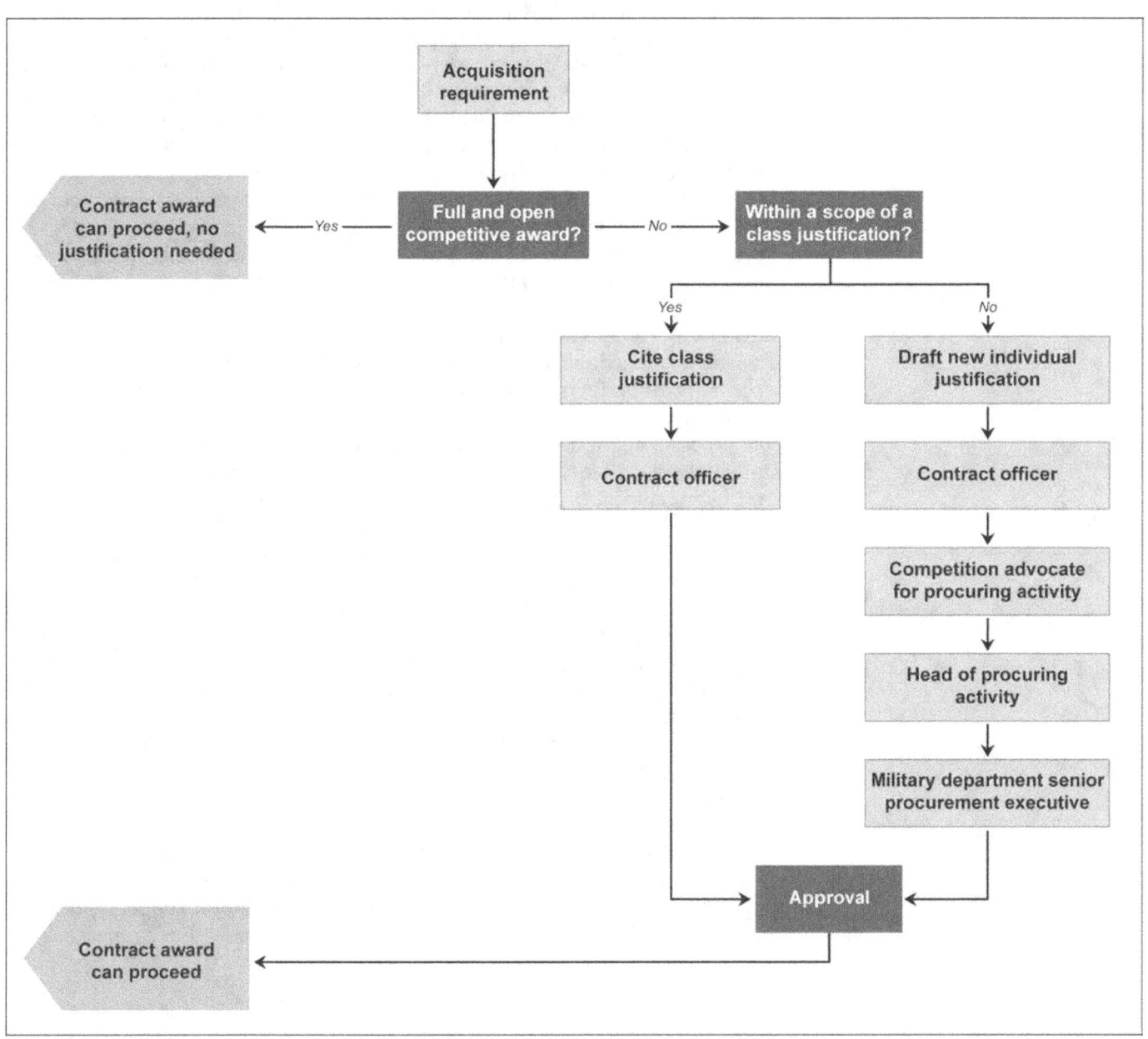

Source: GAO analysis of the Federal Acquisition Regulation.
Note: Initial approval of class justifications is subject to the same process as individual justifications.

GAO-12-263 Defense Contracting

In some cases, the class justifications we reviewed included a list of firms authorized to participate, as well as anticipated obligation amounts for each firm over the applicable time period. For instance, one of the Air Force class justifications we reviewed listed about 40 firms, each with anticipated contract obligations of several million to several billion dollars during the 7-year time frame of the class justification. Despite the number of firms listed in the class justification, competition among them for a given contract award was rare—the contracts we reviewed under this justification typically stated that only one of the firms was capable of meeting the government's requirements. Officials at one Air Force center said that amending their existing class justification to add new firms had proved difficult in the past, and noted that this can reduce competition by limiting ability to work with new entrants to the market.

Some Air Force officials also noted that concerns about the level of review of individual contracts that are awarded without full and open competition under class justifications have led to efforts to revise the review process for activity under class justifications. The Air Force revised its process in a recently approved national security class justification for an intelligence, surveillance, and reconnaissance program office, requiring individual contract actions over $85.5 million be submitted to the Air Force senior procurement executive for expedited review.[11] According to an Air Force General Counsel official, the Air Force has not yet determined what type of documentation will be required as part of that review, but it believes the increased review may identify additional opportunities for competition. This is the first Air Force class justification to include this new process, and officials were not aware of any similar processes at other DOD entities. According to Air Force officials, the new class justification also includes a mechanism for adding new firms after the initial approval of the justification. Officials in the affected program office said that they anticipate an increase in competition rates as a result of this new flexibility.

Regardless of whether the military departments used class or individual justifications, all those we reviewed met FAR standards. We reviewed justification and approval documents for the use of the exception for 27 different contracts awarded by the Army, Navy, and Air Force, and all met

---

[11] This new class justification is the successor to one of the Air Force justifications included in our review.

the standards established in the Federal Acquisition Regulation for approving the justification. In addition, we reviewed the justifications and approval documents for one national security exception contract each at NGA, NRO, and DIA, and two such contracts at NSA, and all generally met the requirements of the FAR.

There Are No Alternative Authorities for National Security Sensitive Procurements, but Additional Exceptions May Be Cited in Some Cases

According to officials from all DOD components we met with, the national security exception should be used in limited circumstances where full and open competition would compromise national security. These officials were not aware of other authorities that could be used in its place, nor were they aware of any such proposed authorities. In some justifications and approval documents, DOD components may cite other exceptions in addition to the national security exception. For example, the entities that reported using the national security exception for all or nearly all contracting—NSA, NRO, and some Air Force SAPs—reported citing additional exceptions when making sole-source contract awards. According to policy documents and officials with these organizations, it is standard practice to list more than one exception when applicable. For example, one NSA contract for computer security equipment that we reviewed cited the "only one responsible source and no other supplies or services will satisfy agency requirements" FAR exception alongside the national security exception, because contracting officials had determined that only one firm was capable of meeting the government's requirements. Likewise, in awarding a satellite contract, NRO used the "only one responsible source" exception in addition to the national security exception. The military departments generally do not cite additional exceptions when using the national security exception.

Level of Competition under the National Security Exception Varied Greatly Within DOD

Few Military Department Contracts Achieved Competition under National Security Exception

According to federal procurement data, the military departments typically did not achieve competition on national security exception contracts. Of the more than 11,300 DOD military department contract actions citing the national security exception from fiscal years 2007 through 2010, DOD received only one proposal for $10.6 billion of its obligations—about 84 percent of the total $12.7 billion in obligations under this exception.[12] About 4 percent of contract actions, which account for 16 percent of the military departments' obligations, received two or more proposals, as shown in figure 7 below. By department, nearly 100 percent of Air Force and 95 percent of Navy contract obligations received only one proposal, whereas about 80 percent of Army obligations were made under contracts that received more than one proposal.[13]

[12] FPDS-NG indicated that about 70 actions accounting for 0.02 percent of obligations (about $3.16 million) under the national security exception at the military departments received no proposals, which are likely data entry errors.

[13] About 87 percent of Army contract actions received only one proposal, but the actions that did receive multiple proposals had much larger obligation amounts, on average.

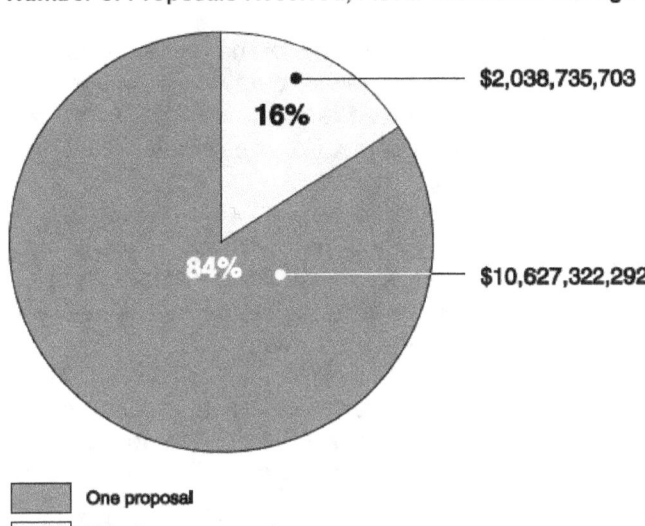

Figure 7: Percentage of total DOD National Security Exception Obligations by Number of Proposals Received, Fiscal Years 2007 through 2010

$2,038,735,703

16%

84%

$10,627,322,292

☐ One proposal

☐ More than one proposal

Source: GAO analysis of FPDS-NG data.

DOD's Better Buying Power Initiative includes a goal of decreasing instances where only one proposal is received, which DOD has noted fails to provide the full benefits of competition. We have previously reported that about 13 percent of all contract obligations governmentwide were made on contracts awarded with competitive procedures that only received one proposal.[14]

Contracts receiving only one proposal are considered competitively awarded if the solicitation was open to multiple potential offerors, so contracts reported in FPDS-NG that received only one proposal may have been awarded using competitive procedures. While data on the extent that national security exception contracts were awarded competitively were not sufficiently reliable, the available data confirmed that competition is infrequent—indicating that less than a quarter of military department obligations under this exception were competitively awarded. Furthermore, our data reliability assessment indicated that the errors in

---

[14] GAO, *Federal Contracting: Opportunities Exist to Increase Competition and Assess Reasons When Only One Offer Is Received*, GAO-10-833 (Washington, D.C.: July 26, 2010).

these data tend to overstate the level of competition, so the actual level may be lower.

Likewise, few of the military department national security exception contracts we reviewed achieved competition. Of the 27 contracts we reviewed for the Air Force, Army, and Navy, only one received multiple proposals. For the remaining 26 contracts, only one proposal for each was received.

Military department officials said that they make efforts to provide competition to the greatest extent practicable, as required by the FAR. However, they reported three obstacles to obtaining more competition in contract awards:

- the existence of a small number of firms able to meet the security requirements for the goods and services being procured;
- constraints on soliciting new vendors, including proprietary data and reliance on incumbent contractor expertise; and
- not having tools to increase market research and solicit vendors in a secure environment.

For example, Air Force contracting officials reported that restrictions on time and expertise make it difficult for many new vendors to meet requirements. A senior Air Force contracting official told us that not having access to technical data—such as engineering drawings and other information needed to have another vendor meet the eligibility requirements—is a major barrier to competition. According to this official, one vendor often controls the data as proprietary information, and buying or recreating it would be cost-prohibitive for potential new vendors.

The military departments generally continue to use the same exception for follow-on contract actions to national security exception contracts, as well as the same vendor, based on our analysis of the contracts in our sample. Contracting officials noted that these contracts must go through the same approval process as the initial contract, requiring justification for the national security exception. Of the 27 contracts in our sample, we identified 14 follow-on contracts, 12 of which were awarded to the incumbent contractor. Contracting officials confirmed that follow-on contracts typically are not competed and are usually awarded to the same vendor due to proprietary data rights and expertise of the incumbent contractors, as well as the time required to initiate work with a new vendor. We have previously reported that incumbent contractors have important advantages in follow-on contract awards.[15]

Contracting officials told us that the tools that are used to solicit competition generally cannot be used in a security sensitive contracting environment. FedBizOpps.com is the military departments' primary tool for soliciting potential offerors.[16] The site allows agencies to upload unclassified solicitations for goods and services, but it cannot accept classified material.[17] Even though national security exception contract documents are often unclassified, synopsizing the requirements may pose a security risk. Instead, contracting officials identify potential sources based on market research and provide the solicitations to those firms directly.

For the 27 contracts in our sample, the market research reflected in the contract files frequently did not have adequate documentation on how it was used to identify potential offerors.[18] Specifically, no evidence of market research was present in 12 of the 27 contract files we reviewed; it was present in 15 of the files we reviewed. The market research in those 15 contracts often broadly outlined the means by which the contracting office conducted the market research, but in some cases did not include details and evidence to document the research. In some cases, the contracting officials relied upon their own collective experience with, and knowledge of, vendors capable of delivering goods and services in accordance with sensitive contract requirements. Nevertheless, even in cases in which market research identified multiple firms that could meet requirements, it did not always result in multiple proposals on a given contract.

---

[15] GAO-10-833.

[16] The FAR requires contracting officers to synopsize proposed contract actions expected to exceed $25,000 in the Government Point of Entry (GPE), *FedBizOpps.com*. FAR § 5.101(a)(1) The GPE may be accessed via the Internet at https://www.fbo.gov/. FAR § 5.201(d).

[17] Contract awards involving classified materials may be announced publicly on FedBizOpps.com in instances where the solicitation itself is unclassified.

[18] The FAR requires that agencies conduct market research to arrive at the most suitable approach to acquiring, distributing, and supporting supplies and services. FAR § 10.000.

DOD Intelligence Agencies Reported High Levels of Competition by Conducting Market Research and Soliciting Proposals within a Secure Environment

NSA and NRO, which reported that they use the national security exception for all or nearly all contracting, showed high levels of competition compared to the DOD military departments. As illustrated in figure 8 below, according to data provided by the agencies, annual competition rates ranged from 27 percent to nearly 70 percent of total obligations at NSA and NRO. Because data on contracting at intelligence agencies are typically classified at highly restrictive levels, we did not have sufficient access to independently validate the data provided.

Figure 8: Reported Percentage of Contract Obligations Awarded Competitively

Percentage of contract obligations awarded competitively

Fiscal year

☐ NRO
■ NSA

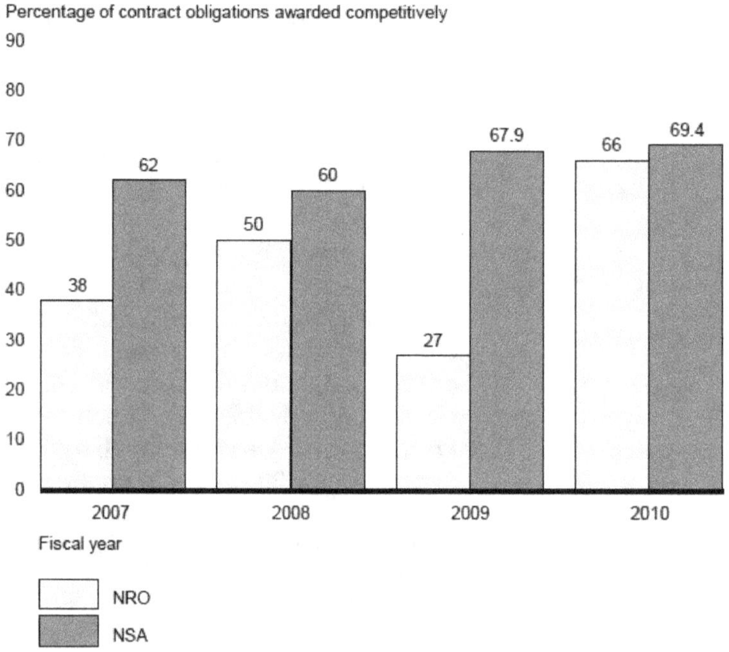

Source: GAO analysis of FPDS-NG data.

NRO and NSA have both developed tools to help increase competition in procuring sensitive goods and services and have made these tools available for other intelligence agencies. These tools bring together a large number of potential offerors and help the agencies solicit and evaluate vendors, and competitively award the contract, while taking measures to limit the risk to national security. The NRO Acquisition Research Center, developed for intelligence community procurements, limits potential contractors to about 1,200 registered firms that are already cleared to perform in a secure environment and have a workforce with security clearances. An NRO senior procurement official described this system as a proprietary classified version of FedBizOpps. The NSA's Acquisition Resource Center is the NSA's business registry database that provides industry with a central source for acquisition information. This system also serves as a market research tool for NSA personnel, as well as a means for distribution of acquisition documents to its industry partners. All companies that wish to do business with NSA must be registered in the system. As of October 2010, the database included about 9,300 companies.[19]

An NSA Inspector General report found that this system improved the agency's ability to conduct market research and solicit competition. The inspector general found that it improved competition by making the process more systematic. The other two DOD intelligence agencies, DIA and NGA, have made arrangements to use one or both of the NSA and NRO systems. For example, our review of a DIA contract under the national security exception showed that the agency solicited 11 companies and received five proposals by using NSA's Acquisition Resource Center. Additionally, NGA has a memorandum of agreement with NRO to use its Acquisition Research Center. None of the 27 military department contracts we reviewed used the NSA or NRO systems to conduct market research. However, contracting officials at one Air Force center said that they were aware of NRO's system, and although they do not currently have access, they would like the opportunity to use it for their procurements.

Conclusions

DOD's use of the national security exception is necessary in certain situations when disclosing the government's needs in a full and open competition would reveal information that would harm national security. The exception requires that agencies pursue limited competition by requesting proposals from as many potential sources as is feasible. DOD departments may not have a complete understanding of the extent of competition, given that DOD lacks clear policy on when sensitive contract actions should be excluded from the FPDS-NG, the database it uses to track this information. However, the available data show that the military departments have achieved relatively little competition in their national security exception procurements. Obtaining competition on new

---

[19] The database includes companies with existing security clearances, as well as companies without clearances.

procurements is especially important, because our findings and previous reports have shown that once a contractor receives an award, historically that contractor is likely to receive any follow-on contract. There are obstacles to competition in sensitive procurements, including a limited number of firms that can meet security requirements. Because of these obstacles, program offices may find it easier to forego competition when a class justification is already in place. However, more competition is possible. The recent changes that Air Force made to its process, which introduced a new high-level review of contract actions under a class justification, may help increase the extent of competition. Further, while the military departments face challenges in conducting market research for sensitive contracts, the DOD intelligence agencies, which face similar challenges, have created tools to increase their ability to identify multiple potential sources and obtain competition when using the national security exception. The use of such tools could enhance the ability of the military departments to obtain competition on their national security exception procurements.

Recommendations for Executive Action

We recommend that the Secretary of Defense take the following three actions:

- Issue guidance establishing the circumstances under which security sensitive contracting data are required to be reported to OSD and in FPDS-NG, including the decision authority for excluding a given program or contract from the database.
- Evaluate the effect of the Air Force's new review process on competition and management oversight of national security exception actions under a class justification; if the changes are found to be beneficial, consider implementing similar changes across DOD.
- Assess the feasibility of providing contracting officials in military department programs that routinely use the national security exception with access to tools that facilitate market research and competitive solicitation in a secure environment, either through development of new tools or access to existing intelligence community systems.

Agency Comments and Our Evaluation

We provided a draft of this report to DOD. In written comments, DOD concurred with the report's last two recommendations and partially concurred with the first recommendation. DOD also provided technical comments, which we incorporated as appropriate. DOD's comments are reprinted in appendix II.

In commenting on the draft report, DOD agreed to evaluate the Air Force's new review process for national security exception actions under class justifications and implement a similar process across the department if it found it beneficial. DOD also agreed to explore deploying existing intelligence community market research and solicitation tools to organizations in the military departments that frequently use the national security exception. DOD partially concurred with our recommendation to clarify guidance on the exclusion of data from FPDS-NG citing a pending revision to the FAR that will clarify that classified data should not be reported to FPDS-NG. We did not encounter any ambiguity on this point—contracting officials we met with were clear that classified data should not be entered into the system. However, we found that DOD policy was not clear on if and when sensitive, but unclassified, contract data should be excluded from FPDS-NG. We continue to believe that additional guidance is needed to clarify if and when any such data should be excluded (outside the existing intelligence agency waiver), and if so, outline the criteria and decision authority for doing so.

We are sending copies of this report to interested congressional committees and the Secretary of Defense. This report will also be available at no charge on GAO's website at http://www.gao.gov.

If you or your staff have any questions about this report or need additional information, please contact me at (202) 512-4841 or martinb@gao.gov. Contact points for our Offices of Congressional Relations and Public Affairs may be found on the last page of this report. Staff acknowledgments are provided in appendix III.

Belva M. Martin
Director
Acquisition and Sourcing Management

List of Committees

The Honorable Carl Levin
Chairman
The Honorable John McCain
Ranking Member
Committee on Armed Services
United States Senate

The Honorable Howard P. "Buck" McKeon
Chairman
The Honorable Adam Smith
Ranking Member
Committee on Armed Services
House of Representatives

Appendix I: Scope and Methodology

Our mandate required us to review (1) the pattern of usage of the national security exception by acquisition organizations within the Department of Defense to determine which organizations are commonly using the exception and the frequency of such usage; (2) the range of items or services being acquired through the use of such exception; (3) the process for reviewing and approving justifications involving such exception; 4) whether the justifications for use of such exception typically meet the requirements of the Federal Acquisition Regulation applicable to the use of such exception; (5) issues associated with follow-on procurements for items or services acquired using such exception; and (6) potential additional instances where such exception could be applied and any authorities available to DOD other than such exception that could be applied in such instances. To respond to these objectives, this report (1) identified the pattern of DOD's use of the national security exception, including the range of goods and services acquired; (2) assessed DOD's process for using this exception; and (3) determined the extent to which DOD obtained competition on selected contracts using the national security exception.

To conduct our work we met with DOD officials at the Office of the Secretary of Defense (OSD), the three military departments, and DOD intelligence agencies. Within OSD we met with Defense Procurement and Acquisition Policy officials, including a Federal Procurement Data System-Next Generation (FPDS-NG) subject-matter expert. We also met with FPDS-NG experts in the three military departments. In addition, across DOD we met with officials from the following offices:

U.S. Air Force

- Office of the Deputy Assistant Secretary for Contracting and Policy
- Air Force Materiel Command, Special Programs Division
- Air Force Materiel Command, Implementation Branch
- General Counsel

U.S. Army

- Office of the Assistant Secretary of the Army for Acquisition, Logistics and Technology
- Army Materiel Command
- Army Contracting Command
- Army Space and Missile Defense Command
- General Counsel

U.S. Navy	• Office of the Assistant Secretary of the Navy, Research, Development & Acquisition • Naval Sea Systems Command • Space and Naval Warfare Systems Command • General Counsel
Defense Intelligence Agency	• Office of Contracting • Office of the Inspector General • General Counsel
National Geospatial-Intelligence Agency	• Acquisition and Contracts Office • Office of the Inspector General • General Counsel
National Security Agency	• Acquisition Organization • Office of Contracting • Office of the Inspector General • General Counsel
National Reconnaissance Office	• Office of Contracting • Office of the Inspector General • General Counsel

Based on discussions with FPDS-NG subject-matter experts at OSD and the three military departments, we determined that the data available prior to fiscal year 2006 were not sufficiently reliable for our purposes. Therefore, our review focused on the most current reliable data from FPDS-NG, fiscal years 2007 through 2010. We conducted legal research and interviewed DOD officials to identify other uses of the exception and alternative authorities. To identify the DOD components to include in our review, we used FPDS-NG data to determine those with the most obligations under the national security exception during fiscal years 2007 through 2010. These included the three military departments—the Air Force, Army, and Navy. Within the departments, we identified the commands with the highest obligations under the exception—the Air Force Materiel Command (AFMC), Army Materiel Command / Army Contracting Command (AMC/ACC), Army Space and Missile Defense Command (SMDC), and Navy's Space and Naval Warfare Systems Command (SPAWAR). For entities that do not report data to FPDS-NG we relied on knowledgeable DOD officials to identify the frequent users of the national security exception. These included the four DOD intelligence agencies—the Defense Intelligence Agency (DIA), National Geospatial-Intelligence Agency (NGA), National Security Agency (NSA), and National

Reconnaissance Office (NRO), as well as Special Access Programs within the DOD military departments. Due to the security limitations at the intelligence agencies, we employed different methodological approaches to assess the uses and processes at the intelligence agencies and the military departments, as described below.

DOD Military Departments

To assess the pattern of use of the exception and the range of items or services being acquired at the DOD military departments, we obtained data from FPDS-NG. We included contracts and orders coded as using the national security exception under the field "reason not competed" from fiscal years 2007 through 2010. We analyzed obligations data and the types of goods and services based on product code fields. To compare use of the national security exception versus other FAR exceptions, we conducted an analysis of the other values listed under the "reason not competed" field.

To determine the processes the military departments employ when using the national security exception and the extent to which they obtain competition, we reviewed DOD policies and guidance and selected contract files based on a non-generalizable sample of 27. The sample included files from the three commands within the military departments with the highest reported percentage of obligations under the exception in fiscal years 2007 through 2010—AFMC, AMC, and SPAWAR.[1] Within these three commands, we identified contracting offices with the highest reported obligations under the national security exception as well as contracting offices with a high percentage of overall contracting dollars obligated under the national security exception. The components we identified for the sample were:

Air Force Materiel Command

- Air Logistics Center, Robins Air Force Base
- Aeronautical Systems Center, Wright-Patterson Air Force Base

Army Materiel Command

- Army Contracting Command, Aberdeen Proving Ground
- Special Operations Command, Ground Application Program Office, Fort Belvoir
- Soldier Systems Center, Natick Army Base

---

[1] Two Army commands made up nearly equal shares of Army's total obligations under the National Security Exception. We selected AMC for review over SMDC for logistical purposes.

Navy Space and Warfare
Systems Command

- Systems Center Charleston

Because the Air Force makes up 73.5 percent of all obligations under the national security exception, we selected 18 contracts from the Air Force, 6 from the Army, and 3 from the Navy. We selected the individual contracts based on several criteria. First, we selected high-dollar contracts. Based on our analysis of commonly procured goods and services from FPDS-NG data, we selected contracts with a mix of these types of purchases. FPDS-NG data do not indicate whether a contract is a follow-on procurement, therefore we selected both older and newer contracts. DOD officials also identified contracts to select to capture follow-on activities. However, based on other selection criteria, these contracts had already been included. The 27 contracts we reviewed represented about $3.4 billion—about 27 percent—of the $12.7 billion in obligations under the national security exception across the military departments in fiscal years 2007 through 2010.

We analyzed the justification and authorization documents for these selected contracts and determined whether they met the requirements of the FAR Sections 6.302-6 and 6.303-2. In addition, we reviewed pre-award documentation to determine the extent to which the services obtained competition under the exception and to review market research documents. Further, we reviewed the contract files to determine whether the contract was a follow-on contract. We met with officials to discuss efforts the military departments make to obtain competition when using the national security exception to limit competition.

We conducted assessments of both the completeness and the reliability of the FPDS-NG data. To assess how complete the FPDS-NG data are, we interviewed agency officials at OSD and the three military departments to identify instances when individual contracts or entire programs are excluded from FPDS-NG to protect classification or security sensitive information. OSD officials provided us with the directive from the Director of National Intelligence that exempts all DOD intelligence agencies from FPDS-NG. We met with officials who oversee Special Access Programs in the Army and Air Force to discuss any policies and procedures related to the inclusion or exclusion of contract information from FPDS-NG.

Our assessment of the reliability of FPDS-NG data involved several stages. First, we interviewed FPDS-NG subject-matter experts at OSD and the three military departments. We discussed issues with miscoding and results of any anomaly reports. After identifying the sample for our file review, we asked officials at the contracting offices to verify if the contracts did use the national security exception as they were coded in the "Reason not Competed" field in FPDS-NG. After identifying coding errors in that field for five of the contracts, we compared the "Extent Competed" and "Number of Bids" (proposals) fields with the documentation in the contract files for the 27 contracts in our review. We found four errors in the "Extent Competed" field and one error in the numbers of proposals. We also drew upon prior GAO findings regarding FPDS-NG data reliability.

Based on this initial data reliability assessment, we selected a second random, non-generalizable stratified sample of 36 contracts to assess the same three fields in FPDS-NG. We stratified based on the military department (Air Force, Army, and Navy); whether it was identified as an indefinite delivery, indefinite quantity contract in FPDS-NG; and whether it was listed as not competed or competed after exclusion of sources in FPDS-NG. We asked DOD officials to review contract files to determine 1) if the contract cited the national security exception, 2) whether the contract was competed, and 3) how many proposals the contract received. In addition, in discussions with the Navy, they identified contracts that were incorrectly coded as using the national security exception. After three Air Force contracts fell out of our sample due to nonresponse, we found errors in the "Extent Competed" field for about a third of the contracts. However, we found only two of the contracts (6 percent) had errors in the "Reason not Competed" field and only one contract (3 percent) with an error in the number of proposals. These data reliability assessments indicate that the "Reason not Competed" and "Number of Offers" fields in FPDS-NG are sufficiently reliable for our analyses.

DOD Intelligence Agencies and Special Access Programs

To assess the extent of DOD intelligence agencies' use of the national security exception, we obtained data from the four agencies, as these agencies do not report data to FPDS-NG. Specifically, we obtained data on the percentage of total obligations under the national security exception and the percentage of total obligations competed at the four agencies.

We reviewed five contract files at four DOD intelligence agencies. We analyzed the justification and authorization documents for these selected contracts and determined whether they met the requirements of the FAR Sections 6.302-6 and 6.303-2. Because we did not have a list of contract numbers from which to choose, we relied on the agencies to select the contracts for review. In addition, we reviewed pre-award documentation to determine the extent to which the agencies obtained competition under the exception and to review market research documents. Further, we reviewed the contract files to determine whether the contract was a follow-on contract. We met with officials to discuss efforts the intelligence agencies make to obtain competition when using the national security exception to limit competition.

DOD entities for which little or no use of the exception appeared in federal procurement data were not included in our file review. To assess the use of the exception at these entities, we met with officials at OSD, as well as officials knowledgeable about Special Access Programs at the Army, Air Force, and Navy. We obtained information from an Air Force official on the extent of use and competition within the Air Force Materiel Command's Special Programs Division.

To assess the reliability of data received from the DOD intelligence agencies, we solicited information from officials on the data. Specifically, we asked cognizant officials about the type of database systems used to track contracting activity; how these systems are used; what procedures are in place to ensure consistency and accuracy; if there have been issues with the system that may compromise data; what limitations exist in tracking CICA exceptions; and what data reliability assessments have been conducted on these systems.

We conducted this performance audit from March 2011 to January 2012 in accordance with generally accepted government auditing standards. Those standards require that we plan and perform the audit to obtain sufficient, appropriate evidence to provide a reasonable basis for our findings and conclusions based on our audit objectives. We believe that the evidence obtained provides a reasonable basis for our findings and conclusions based on our audit objectives.

Appendix II: Comments from the Department of Defense

OFFICE OF THE UNDER SECRETARY OF DEFENSE
3000 DEFENSE PENTAGON
WASHINGTON, DC 20301-3000

ACQUISITION,
TECHNOLOGY
AND LOGISTICS

Ms. Belva M. Martin
Director, Acquisition and Sourcing Management
U.S. Government Accountability Office
441 G Street, N.W.
Washington, DC 20548

JAN 1 1 2012

Dear Ms. Martin:

This is the Department of Defense (DoD) response to the GAO Draft Report, GAO-12-263, "DEFENSE CONTRACTING: Improved Policies and Tools Could Help Increase Competition on DoD's National Security Exception Procurements," dated November 21, 2011 (GAO Code 120965). Detailed comments on the report recommendations are enclosed.

Sincerely,

Richard Ginman
Director, Defense Procurement
and Acquisition Policy

Enclosure:
As stated

GAO Draft Report Dated November 21, 2011
GAO-12-263 (GAO CODE 120965)

"DEFENSE CONTRACTING: IMPROVED POLICIES AND TOOLS COULD HELP
INCREASE COMPETITION ON DOD'S NATIONAL SECURITY EXCEPTION
PROCUREMENTS"

DEPARTMENT OF DEFENSE COMMENTS
TO THE GAO RECOMMENDATIONS

RECOMMENDATION 1: The GAO recommends that the Secretary of Defense issue guidance establishing the circumstances under which security-sensitive contracting data is required to be reported to the Office of the Secretary of Defense (OSD) and in the Federal Procurement Data System – Next Generation (FPDS-NG), including the decision authority for excluding a given program or contract from the database.

DoD RESPONSE: Partially concur. The Defense Federal Acquisition Regulation Supplement (DFARS) Procedures, Guidance, and Information (PGI) 204.606(2)(ii) instructs the Components not to report actions that are classified in FPDS-NG. FAR Case 2010-014, "Updates to Contract Reporting and Central Contractor Registration," (currently out for public comment in Federal Register 76 FR 73564) provides a proposed rule to clarify that FPDS-NG is only for unclassified actions. At the request of the Office of the Director of National Intelligence (ODNI), DPAP granted a waiver to NGA, DIA, and NSA to not report unclassified actions in FDPS-NG due to concerns that aggregation of unclassified contract action data may reveal operational sensitive mission information. The waiver was not granted to address national security issues of a specific program. The NRO was not included in the waiver because its procurement authority does not originate with the DoD. DoD does not intend to grant additional waivers to other DoD organizations for FPDS-NG reporting.

RECOMMENDATION 2: The GAO recommends that the Secretary of Defense evaluate the effect of the Air Force's new review process on competition and management oversight of national security exception actions under a class justification; if the changes are found to be beneficial, consider implementing similar changes DoD.

DoD RESPONSE: Concur. The Department will evaluate the Air Force review process, and if determined to be beneficial, will prepare guidance to implement a similar process throughout the DoD.

RECOMMENDATION 3: The GAO recommends that the Secretary of Defense assess the feasibility of providing contracting officials in military department programs that routinely use the national security exception with access to tools that facilitate market research and competitive solicitation in a secure environment, either through development of new tools or access to existing intelligence community systems.

DoD RESPONSE: Concur. The Department will assess existing intelligence community market research tools, and if feasible will provide the military departments using the National Security exception at FAR 6.302-6 access to the market research tools to help improve competition in a secure environment.

Appendix III: GAO Contact and Staff Acknowledgments

GAO Contact	Belva M. Martin, (202) 512-4841 or martinb@gao.gov
Staff Acknowledgments	In addition to the contact named above, John Neumann, Assistant Director; Laura Greifner; Julia M. Kennon; John A. Krump; Caryn E. Kuebler; Teague Lyons; Jean McSween; Kenneth Patton; Roxanna T. Sun; Sonya Vartivarian; and C. Patrick Washington made key contributions to this report.

GAO's Mission	The Government Accountability Office, the audit, evaluation, and investigative arm of Congress, exists to support Congress in meeting its constitutional responsibilities and to help improve the performance and accountability of the federal government for the American people. GAO examines the use of public funds; evaluates federal programs and policies; and provides analyses, recommendations, and other assistance to help Congress make informed oversight, policy, and funding decisions. GAO's commitment to good government is reflected in its core values of accountability, integrity, and reliability.
Obtaining Copies of GAO Reports and Testimony	The fastest and easiest way to obtain copies of GAO documents at no cost is through GAO's website (www.gao.gov). Each weekday afternoon, GAO posts on its website newly released reports, testimony, and correspondence. To have GAO e-mail you a list of newly posted products, go to www.gao.gov and select "E-mail Updates."
Order by Phone	The price of each GAO publication reflects GAO's actual cost of production and distribution and depends on the number of pages in the publication and whether the publication is printed in color or black and white. Pricing and ordering information is posted on GAO's website, http://www.gao.gov/ordering.htm. Place orders by calling (202) 512-6000, toll free (866) 801-7077, or TDD (202) 512-2537. Orders may be paid for using American Express, Discover Card, MasterCard, Visa, check, or money order. Call for additional information.
Connect with GAO	Connect with GAO on Facebook, Flickr, Twitter, and YouTube. Subscribe to our RSS Feeds or E-mail Updates. Listen to our Podcasts. Visit GAO on the web at www.gao.gov.
To Report Fraud, Waste, and Abuse in Federal Programs	Contact: Website: www.gao.gov/fraudnet/fraudnet.htm E-mail: fraudnet@gao.gov Automated answering system: (800) 424-5454 or (202) 512-7470
Congressional Relations	Katherine Siggerud, Managing Director, siggerudk@gao.gov, (202) 512-4400, U.S. Government Accountability Office, 441 G Street NW, Room 7125, Washington, DC 20548
Public Affairs	Chuck Young, Managing Director, youngc1@gao.gov, (202) 512-4800 U.S. Government Accountability Office, 441 G Street NW, Room 7149 Washington, DC 20548

www.ingramcontent.com/pod-product-compliance
Lightning Source LLC
Chambersburg PA
CBHW080922290526
45795CB00007BA/2614